AN OUTLINE OF ICIBEMBA GRAMMAR

MICHAEL MANN

Series Editor: MUBANGA KASHOKI

Bookworld Publishers

First published in 1977 by the Institute for African Studies (now the Institute of Economic and Social Research), University of Zambia in *Language in Zambia: Grammatical Sketches.*

This edition published by Bookworld Publishers
PO Box 32581, Lusaka, Zambia.
1999

ISBN 9982 24 0145

Typesetting by Fergan Limited, Lusaka, Zambia.

Printed by Printech Limited, Lusaka, Zambia

FOREWORD

There has long been a lack of up to date descriptive grammars of Zambian languages suitable for use, either as teaching or as learning aids, at all levels of the Zambian education system. This lack has been keenly felt by teachers and learners alike. Many of the grammars that are available could be said to be inadequate or inappropriate in several respects. The oldest ones were written at a time when Latin or European languages generally were considered to be the prototype of all grammars, and thus they tended to be patterned in their arrangement, description and the terminology employed on Latin-based grammatical rules. Others were written in a style and language which presented serious problems of comprehension even to teachers. In a good many cases, the actual examples cited were unnatural, forced or not in accord with accepted usage. At the present moment many of these works have long been out of print.

In order to put in the hands of the teachers and learners grammatical descriptions which reflected more nearly the structural facts of their language, during 1970-71, the Survey of Language Use and Language Teaching in Zambia attempted to provide comprehensible grammatical descriptions of the seven Zambian languages officially prescribed for use in education, broadcasting and literacy programmes. The authors who volunteered or were approached to write them were specifically instructed to employ a comprehensible style and to keep technical terminology to the absolute minimum. The general reader was clearly in mind. It is hoped that with the publishing now of the grammatical outlines of iciBemba, siLozi, ciNyanja and chiTonga the original intention of providing grammatical descriptions of appeal to a wide audience, both lay and professional, will have been achieved.

As originally conceived, seven grammatical sketches representing all the seven officially approved Zambian languages, plus sketches of Town Bemba and Town Tonga, were to have been published as Part One in a projected three-part volume of **Language in Zambia,** incorporating the findings of the Zambia

Language Survey. In the event, it was found necessary in the interest of reducing bulk and cost to abandon the original plan and to arrange to publish the sketches separately. Indeed, publishing them separately has the advantage of making them available in a convenient, less bulky size suitable for both teacher and student handling.

The Institute for African Studies (now the Institute of Economic and Social Research), University of Zambia, published in 1977 **Language in Zambia: Grammatical Sketches,** Volume 1, containing grammatical sketches or outlines of iciBemba and kiKaonde by Michael Mann and JL Wright respectively, plus a sketch of the main characteristics of Town Bemba by Mubanga E Kashoki. The plan at the time was to publish subsequently two follow-up volumes: first, Volume 2, to contain sketches of siLozi and Lunda and Luvale and second, Volume 3, to contain sketches of ciNyanja and chiTonga. In the event this plan was not adhered to. Only one volume was published in accordance with the original plan and this has been out of print for some time now.

It is in part for these reasons that it has been considered necessary to attend to the unfinished business initiated some two decades ago. Also, and more pertinently, the need for pedagogical and reference grammars of Zambian languages continues to be keenly felt. The matter has now been made more urgent following the recent (1996) decision of the Zambian Government to revert to the earlier policy of using local (i.e. Zambian) languages plus English as media of instruction. As now re-arranged, in order to achieve what is felt to be a more logical arrangement, four grammatical sketches of iciBemba, siLozi, ciNyanja and chiTonga will be published separately beginning with the present volume containing a grammatical outline of iciBemba.

Co-sponsored by the Institute for African Studies, (the present Institute of Economic and Social Research University of Zambia), the main volume **Language in Zambia,** was published in 1978 by the International African Institute (IAI) partly subsidised by funds from the Ford Foundation. The Institute gratefully acknowledges the permission granted by the Foundation, the sponsors of the language survey of which the material published herein is a partial outcome, to have the sketches published separately. Gratitude is also due to the authors of the sketches for their contribution in a field in which much remains to be done.

Other acknowledgements are due to Bookworld Publishers for publishing the sketches in collaboration with the Institute; to the editors of **Language in Zambia,** Sirarpi Ohannesssian and Mubanga E. Kashoki, for carrying out the bulk of the necessary initial editorial work; to Dr. Tom Gorman who was detailed to bring a general stylistic consistency to the sketches; and to the secretarial Institute staff for preparing the typescript. Above all, the eventual publication of the sketches owes much to the Zambian Government, in particular the Ministry of Education, and to the University of Zambia for their interest and support and for providing a conducive environment in which fruitful research work could take place during the life of the Survey of Language Use and Language Teaching in Zambia.

Mubanga E. Kashoki
Professor of African Languages
INSTITUTE OF ECONOMIC AND SOCIAL RESEARCH
UNIVERSITY OF ZAMBIA
EDITOR

INTRODUCTION

IciBemba, known in English as Bemba or Chibemba, is the principal language of the Northern and Luapula provinces of Zambia, and extends into the Shaba Province of the Democratic Republic of the Congo. It is used in education throughout both provinces in Zambia, but other languages are spoken to the north and east and around Lake Bangweulu, including Bisa, Inamwanga, Mambwe and Tabwa. It has become the common language of the Copperbelt, and is widely spoken in other line-of-rail towns, although there is a noticeable difference between the iciBemba spoken there and that of the villages. The iciBemba described in this outline is the language of the villages sometimes referred to as rural Bemba.

ACKNOWLEDGEMENT

The author has learnt much about iciBemba from the studies of Professor Malcolm Guthrie and Dr. J.C. Sharman, and from many Zambian friends.

Chapter 1
SOUNDS

In this outline we are trying to describe how iciBemba is spoken, not how it is written, although in spelling the sounds we have tried to keep as close as possible to the letters generally used for writing iciBemba. A few spellings may seem strange to Zambians used to reading iciBemba, for instance letters that we have written double like *aa* in *amaano* 'wisdom' and *mm* in *immono* 'castor-oil berries', or the marks we have used to show the way the voice goes up and down. The main reason we have used such spellings is to enable readers who don't know iciBemba to understand exactly how the language is spoken. This does not mean that what we have written is the best way of spelling iciBemba; no language is normally written exactly as it is spoken, but people who know the language can usually read it easily enough. (English spelling is often quite different from the way English is spoken, but not many languages have spelling as difficult as English).

CONSONANTS

The sounds that are written *a, e, i, o,* and *u* are called vowels; *y* and *w* are semi-vowels; all other sounds are called consonants.

The sounds written *m, n, η* and *ny* are a special sort of consonant called **nasals**. When there is another consonant after them, the two sounds together are called a **nasal compound**. Nasals are the only consonants that can have another consonant after them in iciBemba without a vowel in between. English words used in iciBemba often have extra vowels inserted, e.g. *isukulu* 'school', *ubulangeeti*, 'blanket', although Bemba who know English may pronounce them in the English way.

The table below shows the simple consonants and nasal compounds that are used in iciBemba. The reasons why they have been put in columns like this will be explained later, and so will the double spellings *mm, nn, ηη* and *nny*.

1

SIMPLE CONSONANTS			NASAL COMPOUNDS		
b	*belameeni*	hide	**mb**	*mbelame*	should I hide
	bombeeni	work	**mm**	*(mmombe)*	should I work
p	*pepeeni*	pray	**mp**	*mpepe*	should I pray
f	*fumeeni*	leave	**mf**	*mfume*	should I leave
l	*lyeeni*	eat	**nd**	*ndye*	should I eat
	lembeeni	write	**nn**	*(nnembe)*	should I write
t	*tampeeni*	begin	**nt**	*ntampe*	should I begin
s	*sendameeni*	go to sleep	**ns**	*nsendame*	should I go to sleep
sh	*shimyeeni*	put out the light	**nsh**	*nshimye*	should I put out the light
k	*konkeeni*	follow	**nk**	*nkonke*	should I follow
c	*cindeeni*	dance	**nc**	*ncinde*	should I dance
m	*moneeni*	look	**mm**	*mmone*	should I see
n	*nweeni*	drink	**nn**	*nnwe*	should I drink
ŋ	*ŋwintukeeni*	go far away	**ŋŋ**	*ŋŋwintuke*	should I go far away
ny	*nyongeeni*	throttle	**nny**	*nnyonge*	should I throttle
	oweeni	have a bath	**ng**	*ngowe*	should I have a bath
	umfweeni	listen	**nn**	*(ŋŋumfwe)*	should I listen
	ipusheeni	ask	**nj**	*njipushe*	should I ask
	imbeeni	sing	**nny**	*(nnyimbe)*	should I sing

Several sounds have a special pronunciation:

b by itself (but not after *m*) is a **voiced bilabial fricative phonetic** - it is like a *v* sound except that the lips are put almost together as if for an English *b*.

l by itself is an **alveolar flap** (phonetic *l*) - the tongue is flicked rapidly through the position for pronouncing an *l* or *r*; an English person in listening will hesitate over whether he has heard an *l*, an *r* or a *d*. When a nasal comes in front, the sound is written (and pronounced) *nd*; (*l* and *d* are varieties of the same sound in iciBemba).

s always becomes *sh* before an *i* or *y* sound, so that really *s* and *sh* are

2

varieties of the same sound in iciBemba. It even becomes *sh* before *e* when the *e* runs together with a following vowel to make a sound beginning *y*, for instance, *mukeese uluceelo*, 'come in the morning', is pronounced *mukeesh(y)oluceelo*.

c   is pronounced like *ch* in English 'church' (phonetic *t͡s*).

η   is a **velar nasal** - it is the sound represented by *ng* in English 'singer'. It is sometimes spelt *ng'* or in other Zambian languages as *ñ*.

The examples in the table above have been chosen to show some important things about the way sounds change in iciBemba. Bemba words are made up of many parts. The examples on the left are orders or imperatives, made up of the verb root (such as *belam-*, *konk-*) and the ending *–eeni*. There are examples beginning with each of the simple consonants, and four examples beginning with vowels. The examples on the right are made up of the same verb roots and the ending *-e*, with the subject pronoun for 'I, me' in front. They all begin with nasal compound consonants, including those that begin with a vowel in the examples on the left.

The pronoun for 'I, me' is always represented by a nasal consonant, but it is spelt sometimes *m*, sometimes *n*, sometimes *η*, according to the following consonant (see examples in the table above). Linguists will recognise that this is a **homorganic nasal**, pronounced with the tongue and lips in the same position as for the following consonant.

Where the verb root begins with a vowel or semivowel, *g* or *j* are inserted.
g before *o*, *u* or *w*,
j before *e*, *i* or *y*; for instance:

ng-owe	should I swim
ng-ube	should I shelter
ng-we	should I fall over
nj-eshe	should I try
nj-ipushe	should I ask

nje (from *nj-ye)*   should I go.

Before *a,* some speakers say *g,* others *j;* for instance:

njafweeniko or *ngafweeniko*   help me

It should be noted that *g* and *j* only occur after a nasal in iciBemba.

Similar sound changes occur also in nouns, as many nouns have a prefix with a homorganic nasal in their plural form:

ulwala	finger-nail	*ingala*	finger-nails
ulwela	key of kalimba or hand piano	*injela*	keys

In the table on page 2, the way *mmone, nnwe, ŋŋwintuke* and *nnyonge* are spelt in the right hand column is not the usual spelling in Zambia. The first letter has been written twice to show that the syllable before is always long, just as it is before an ordinary nasal compound, for instance:

ka-mmone 'let me see' and *ka-mpepe* 'let me pray', begin with a long syllable but *ka-* is short in *ka-tupepe* 'let us pray' and in the imperative *ka-mone* 'go and see'.

The four other examples, in brackets in the table above, that begin with a double nasal (*mmombe, nnembe, ŋŋumfwe* and *nnyimbe)* have verb roots that normally begin with *b, l* or a vowel or semivowel, as in the imperative examples on the left. We find *mm* instead of *mb,* and the similar changes *nn* instead of *nd, ŋŋ* instead of *ng, nny* instead of *nj* when the next syllable has a nasal compound, and in some words also when the next consonant is a single nasal. The syllable before the double nasal is always long, for instance in *ka-mmombe* 'let me work'. Similar sound changes take place with nouns having a prefix with a homorganic nasal in their plural form:

ulubansa	court-yard	*imbansa*	→	*immansa*	court-yards
ululamba	river-bank	*indamba*	→	*innamba*	river-banks
uluuni	honey-guide bird	*inguni*	→	*iŋŋuni*	honey-guide birds
ulwimbo	song	*injimbo*	→	*innyimbo*	songs

4

In this outline we have used a capital N to spell this homorganic nasal wherever it occurs at the end of a pronoun or prefix to indicate that it may be m, n or η and that it may cause changes in the following consonant.

VOWELS

The vowels in iciBemba are written a, e, i, o and u. The way they are pronounced is much the same as in other Zambian languages (and the same as linguists generally mean by these letters), but they are a little different from the sounds in English. Readers who speak only English will find the vowels sound rather like the vowels in the following English words:

a somewhere between the vowels in cat and cart,

e between mate and met,

i as in meat,

o between coat and cot and

u as in cool.

Many English vowels are diphthongs, i.e. they glide from one vowel sound to another. For instance, 'how' sounds something like *hau;* Bemba vowels are spoken with the tongue still (they are **monophthongs**). When two vowels do come together in Bemba speech, as in the word *ulubao*, 'plank', they belong to different syllables. Bemba vowels are sometimes written double - *aa*, *oo* etc.; this is simply to show that they take longer to say, as is explained a little further on. It is not like the double vowels in English spelling, which often mean that the vowel sounds quite different, for instance, *hop* and *hoop*, *met* and *meet*.

Every word in iciBemba ends in a vowel, and very many words begin with a vowel. In most cases, instead of saying the two vowels that come together one after the other, they run together to make a single sound, for instance *baashita ubwalwa* 'they bought beer' is pronounced, *baashitoobwalwa*. Here are some examples showing how the vowels are pronounced when they run together:

	a + a = aa		*a + i = ee*
e.g.	*akalimba aka*	e.g.	*icilola ici*
pronounced	*akalimbaaka*	pronounced	*iciloleeci*

5

	this instrument			this mirror

a + u = oo

e.g. *umukaka uyu*

pronounced *umukakooyu*

this milk

e + a = yaa

e.g. *abaaume aba*

pronounced *abaumyaaba*

these men

e + i = ee

e.g. *icitele ici*

pronounced *iciteleeci*

this hen-house

e + u = yoo

e.g. *umutete uyu*

pronounced *umutetyooyu*

this straw

i + a = yaa

e.g. *akaabati aka*

pronounced *akaabatyaaka*

this cupboard

i + i = ii

e.g. *icituli ici*

pronounced *icituliici*

this gun

i + u = yuu

e.g. *ulupili ulu*

pronounced *ulupilyuulu*

this hill

o + a = wa

e.g. *akapaaso aka*

pronounced *akapaaswaka*

this grasshopper

o + i = we

e.g. *icikopo icī*

pronounced *icikopweci*

this tin

o + u = oo

e.g. *umulimo uyu*

pronounced *umulimooyu*

this work

u + a = wa

e.g. *abasungu aba*

pronounced *abasungwaba*

these Europeans

u + i = wi

e.g. *icishimu ici*

pronounced *icishimwici*

this caterpillar

u + u = uu

e.g. *ulubafu ulu*

pronounced *ulubafuulu*

this rib

When the first word has *y* or *w* before the last vowel, the sound heard when the vowels run together may be a little different, for instance *mukolwe uyu* 'this cockerel' is pronounced *mukolwoyu*, not **mukolwyooyu*, because iciBemba doesn't have *w* and *y* together. This is how the vowels run together after *w* and *y* although this may not be standard practice:

wa+a=wa we+a=wa wi+a=wa ya+a=yaa ye+a=yaa yo+a=yaa

wa+i=we we+i=we wi+i=wi ya+i=yee ye+i=yee yo+i=yee yu+i=wi

wa+u=wo we+u=wo wi+u=uu ya+u=yoo ye+u=yoo yo+u=yoo yu+u=yu

There are also some rare instances when the normal rules of fusion are not realised in actual speech as expected, for instance:

<blockquote>
(i) **wi + u** which becomes **yuu** instead of ***wyuu**

and

(ii) **yu + i** which becomes **wi** instead of ***ywii**
</blockquote>

e.g., (i) **cimbwi uyu** becomes **cimbyuuyu**

(ii) **icipyu ilyo** caamwikeete aaleefwaya ukufwa becomes **icipwilyo** caamwikeete aaleefwaya ukufwa.

Vowels run together in a similar way between different parts of a word, for instance, *amoolu* 'legs' is made from the prefix *ama-* and the stem *-ulu*. Here are some more examples in which the prefix runs together with the stem:

a + a = aa	a + e = ee	a + i = ee	a + o = oo	a + u = oo
amaato	*abeeni*	*ameeno*	*boonse*	*amoolu*
(ama+ato)	(aba+eni)	(ama+ino)	(ba+onse)	(ama+ulu)
boats	guests	teeth	everyone	legs

i + a = yaa	i + e = yee	i + i = ii	i + o = yoo	i + u = yuu
ilyaashi	*imyeele*	*iliino*	*imyoono*	*ifyuuni*
(ili+ashi)	(imi+ele)	(ili+ino)	(imi+ono)	(ifi+uni)
conversation	knives	tooth	fishtraps	birds

---

where * stands for non-occurrence in the language.

u + a = wa	u + e = we	u + i = wi	u + o = oo	u + u = uu
ubwato	*umweni*	*umwine*	*umoono*	*ukuulu*
(ubu+ato)	(umu+eni)	(umu+ine)	(umu+ono)	(uku+ulu)
boat	guest	owner	fishtrap	leg

Note that *c*, *j* and *sh* already contain a *y* sound (they are **palatalised**). In the conventional spelling, *y* is not written after these letters, so that instead of *icyalo* 'country' it is usual to write *icalo,* (or better as in the 1977 orthography *icaalo* to show the *a* is long). Similarly, many Bemba will run vowels together after these sounds according to the rules given above for words ending *ye*, *ya*, *yo* and *yu*. Thus *iliipusho ili* 'this question' is pronounced *iliipush(y)eli* as if *iliipusho* ended *-shyo*, although some in the Chinsali district may say *iliipushweli*.

When two vowels run together in the middle of a word, the sound that results is always long. When the two vowels belong to different words, for most Bemba speakers the sound is still long, but some in the Luapula valley (and Lubumbashi) pronounce it short.

Vowels do not run together when there is a pause in speech, as at the end of a clause, where one would write a comma. There are also some places where they never run together, for instance:

> *ulya*, 'that', never runs together with the word in front (*Umwaice ulya,* 'that child', is pronounced as two separate words, not *umwaicoolya).*
> Similarly, *ama+insa* is pronounced *amainsa.*

When necessary, we have shown that two vowels do not run together by putting an apostrophe in between them like this:

> *umwaice 'ulya,*
> *ama 'insa,*
> *balee 'endesha*
> *imbeketi i'i 'iisuma*

The spelling with an apostrophe is not used in Zambia, but Zambians do often write a *y* between two vowels, especially when two *a*'s come together, for instance:

8

aayasuka 'he answered'

and sometimes *baleeyendesha* or *iyi* (for *i'i*)

This *y* is what is called a **glide-sound**. It is liable to disappear in other forms of the word, for instance, in the infinitive form *ukwasuka*. Similarly the *y* in *ukufwaya*, 'to look for' disappears in *twafwaile*, 'we looked for'. In this outline we have sometimes spelt this glide-sound *y* to show its special character, e.g. *aay'asuka*.

Most Zambians write iciBemba with the vowels as they sound run together. If a vowel at the end of one word runs together with a following vowel, the sound is written as part of the first word: for instance *ukufula isembe*, 'to forge an axe', is often written *ukufule sembe*. But according to the present (1977) orthography the vowels have now to be written separately between words, and this is what we have done in this outline. In the middle of words we have written the vowels as they sound, except where we have put hyphens to show the separate parts of the word.

LENGTH AND TONE

There are three ways in which languages make some syllables of a word more prominent than others: a syllable may take longer to say, it may be said louder, or it may be said on a higher musical note. English makes one syllable in each word especially prominent by saying it louder and a little longer and higher (saying it with stress). IciBemba does not use stress, but it uses length and musical note (which linguists call tone). It is not just one syllable in each word that may be made long or high, it may be any number or none at all. These differences are one of the main reasons why English people often pronounce iciBemba badly, and why Zambians sometimes find English pronunciation hard.

We can hear the difference of length if we compare *ukupela*, 'to finish', (four short syllables) with *ukupeela*, 'to give', or *ukupenda*, 'to count', (short+short+long+short). Someone not used to hearing length may find that it helps to tap the rhythm.

9

A syllable before a nasal compound is always long;

A syllable containing the semi-vowels *y* or *w* is normally long e.g. *ukupyana*, 'to succeed to', except at the end of a word. However, a vowel after *y* may sometimes be long and sometimes short as in *ukupyaana* (long) and *yaba* (short), 'expressions of impatience, or annoyance', or *yasuka*, (short), 'answer'. If there is neither a semi-vowel nor a following nasal compound, the syllable may be long or short, depending on the length of the vowel.

If the vowel (and syllable) are short, it is written once; if they are long, the vowel is written twice. There is no need to write the vowel twice before a nasal compound or after a *w*, because the syllable is long anyway.

Syllables do not become extra long if there is both a semi-vowel and following nasal compound. *Ukupyanga*, 'to sweep', is simply short+short+long+short. Long vowels are often not shown in the way iciBemba is spelt in Zambia.

Tone changes can be heard in some words like *ámacúngwa*, 'oranges', (low+high+low+high) or, *ulúfungúlo*, 'key', (low+high+low+high+low). Linguists usually write the tones by putting an acute accent on any high tones, and leaving the low tones unmarked, e.g.: *ámacúngwa, ulúfungúlo*. There are often words which are similar in every other way, and are usually spelt the same, but which have different tones and a different meaning, for instance:

ulúkungú	dust	*ulúkúngú*	verandah
ífumo	spear	*ifúmó*	stomach, womb
umúténgó	price	*úmuténgo*	forest patch.

There are examples on page 33 of verb-forms which also have different tones and different meanings. Every word in iciBemba has its proper tones, although there are not always similar words with different tones. It is not possible to speak iciBemba correctly unless each word is said with its proper tones.

What we have called the high tone is not always the same musical note. If the tone has gone from high to low in a word, and then goes up again, it does not go so high. For instance *ámacúngwa* is heard as high+low+middle+low, but a high is always higher than the low tones. Also high tones tend to get lower towards the end of a sentence, and the last high tones may not be heard as being any different from the preceding low tones.

Some long syllables in iciBemba have a tone which starts high and then falls to low, for instance:

naatufika, 'we've arrived', is pronounced falling+middle+low+low
kwali 'there were' is pronounced falling+middle.

The falling tone is written with an acute on the first vowel (if the vowel is written twice), for instance, *náatúfika*, otherwise with a circumflex accent, for instance *kwâlí*. After a falling tone, syllables marked as high are heard with middle tone, just as when the tone has gone from high to low on separate syllables.

Sometimes the tone goes down from high to middle without any low tone in between, for instance, *icungwa*, 'orange' is pronounced high+middle+low. In this outline we have used the mark ! (for instance *i!cungwa*) to show a change from high tone to middle tone without a low tone in between. This is called **tone-slip**.

When two vowels run together *between words*, the tone is high unless both the separate vowels are low. In the examples below, it is only the last one that is pronounced with a low tone between the words:

tuléelyá ámale	*tuléélima ámale*
pronounced *tuleelyaamale*	pronounced *tuleelimaamale*
we are eating millet	we are hoeing millet
tuléelyá amásaká	*tuléélima amásaká*
pronounced *tuléelyáámásaká*	pronounced *tuleelimaamasaka*
we are eating sorghum	we are hoeing sorghum

The real tones of the verbs can be seen when the next word begins with a consonant, for instance:

tuléelyá kalundwé	*tuléélima kalundwé*

we are eating cassava   we are hoeing cassava.

We have spelt the tones on each word as if the vowels did not run together. If two vowels run together in the middle of a word, the rules are very complicated, and in this grammar we have simply tried to show the tones that are actually heard in words made up of different parts.

There is an alternative way of writing the tones (not used in this outline) which Zambians or others may find easier if they are trying to write down the way the language sounds: use a line sloping up between the letters when there is a change from low to high, and sloping down when there is a change from high to low. When the tone goes from high to mid, write a line sloping down and then up, to indicate that the tone has, as it were, gone down and up again. So you would write *u/lu\fun/gun\lo, a\ma/cun\gwa, i\cun\gwa*. Falling tone can be indicated *na\a/tu\fika, or less exactly, naa\tu\fika.*

Chapter 2
NOMINALS

Several points need explanation before we describe the different forms of words in iciBemba. Firstly, we shall talk about nouns and verbs and adjectives, but this does not mean that these terms have exactly the same meaning when they are applied to Bemba words as when they are applied to English, or that an English noun will always be translated by a Bemba noun. Here are three phrases in English and iciBemba:

a tall man	*umúntú úmutali*
a rich man	*umúntú ú!wafyumá*
a famous man	*umúntú úwaishíbíkwá*

Tall, rich and famous are all adjectives in English, and so is *úmutali* in iciBemba. But *ú!wáfyumá* is made from a noun (*ifyumá*, riches), and *úwaishibikwá* is made from a verb (*ukwishibikwa*, become well-known.) There is another difference too. We could have written *úmutali* by itself, meaning a tall person, so that it would correspond to an English noun phrase. As a result, if we are describing iciBemba as it is (and not just the ways in which it is like English), we will have to use some special terms as well as the familiar terms. For instance; **nominal** means any sort of word made from a noun or adjective *(umúntú, úmutali* and *ú!wáfyumá* are all nominals). **Verbal** means any kind of word made from a verb.

There are two special kinds of word made from a verb that are in some ways like nominals, one is the participle (like *úwaíshíbíkwá*), the other the infinitive (like *úkwishíbá*), and they are called **nominal-verbals**.

A second point will already have been noticed by Zambian readers. We have just written *ú!wáfyumá* as one word, although many Zambians would write *uwa fyuma,* and some would even write *uwa ishibikwa.* There are many other cases where we will write a single word where Zambians often divide it up into two or more. The way we have put words together is the one which we feel makes it easiest to explain the grammar of iciBemba, and agrees most closely with where Bemba-speakers will naturally pause in speech. In ordinary speech, however, people do not pause after every word, but only at the end of a clause, so the space left between words in writing makes no difference to the way the language is spoken.

Readers who are unfamiliar with iciBemba or other Bantu languages should note that every noun belongs to a class (most nouns show what class they belong to by a prefix, i.e. by the way they begin), and any word which agrees with it (adjectives, verbs and some other kinds of word) has a prefix at the beginning or an 'infix' in the middle or a special form according to the class of the noun. For instance:

> *icuuni cilya naacímwéne cíléelíísha ákaaná káácíko* 'that bird I saw it yesterday feeding its chick' - *icúúní* 'bird' *(ici-uni)* has agreeing with it:-
> an adjective, *ci-lyá*, 'that',
> a verbal subject pronoun, *cí-léelíísha*, 'it is feeding',
> a verbal object pronoun, *naa-cí-mwéne*, 'I saw it',
> a special possessive form, *káá-cí-ko*, 'its',
> the prefix of the possessive form agrees with *áka-aná*, 'young'

Nouns that have a singular and plural make the plural by changing to another class (which may mean a change in their prefix). For instance, if the above sentence were made plural, it would be:

ifyúúní filyá naafímwéne filéeliísha útwaná twáfiko.

ifyúúní has the prefix *ifi-*, the plural corresponding to *ici-*,

útwaná has *utu-* corresponding to *aka-*

The other words have changed their forms in agreement with the nouns.

STABLE AND UNSTABLE FORMS

Nouns, adjectives and other nominals often change their form according to the job they do in the sentence. For instance,

when *icípushí*, 'pumpkin', is the subject of a sentence, as in *icípushí cáalíbólá*, 'the pumpkin is rotten', its prefix is *ici-;*

but if we make the noun do the work of a verb (make it predicative or copulative) the prefix takes a different form - it may be *cii-*, as in *cilyá cíípushí*, 'that thing is a pumpkin',

or it may be *eci-* or *teeci-* as in *ecípushí*, 'that's the pumpkin', *múngu, teecípushí*, 'it's a gourd, not a pumpkin'.

These forms, used when the nominal is doing the work of a verb, are called **stable forms**. For some nominals the ordinary stable form begins with *ni-*, which is often written as a separate word in Zambia (so are *e-* and *tee-*).

Other forms are called **unstable forms**. Some nominals, but not all, have two unstable forms.

The form used in *icípushí cáalíbólá* (with the prefix *ici-*) is the full form.

The short form is especially found after negative verbs, for instance:

nshílyá cipushí, 'I don't eat pumpkin', with the prefix *ci-*.

Certain nominals may have the short form when they follow a noun and are used to restrict its meaning, for instance:-

ábalúméndo bashíkwête ncínga bááyá pánshi, 'those young men who hadn't got bicycles went on foot'.

We could however have said *abashíkwété* with only slight change in the meaning: the young men, those of them who hadn't got bicycles, went on foot.

14

TONE GROUPS

In the last section we talked about the high, low and middle tones that are heard on different syllables. In this section and the next one we have to explain the particular sequences or tone-patterns that are heard on different kinds of words.

The four sentences below are the same except for the second word (describing what is bought), but each has a different tone-pattern on the second word.

naashíta umúpení mwíshitóóló	I bought a knife in the shop
naashíta úmucélé mwíshitóóló	I bought salt in the shop
naashíta ámacúngwa mwíshitóóló	I bought oranges in the shop
naashíta icísóté mwíshitóóló	I bought a hat in the shop.

There are other words such as *amálayá*, 'shirts', that show the same tone-pattern as *umúpení*, 'knife', so we say that *umúpení* and *amálayá* belong to the same tone-group. Here are some more nouns that belong to the same tone-groups as the nouns in the sentence above:

1	2	3	4
umú-pení	*úmu-célé*	*áma-cúngwa*	*icí-sóté*
knife	salt	oranges	hat
amá-layá	*úmu-píní*	*úmu-kááte*	*umú-píká*
shirts	axe-handle	bread	saucepan
umú-saalú	*úlu-kású*	*áma-lúti*	*umú-pílá*
greens	hoe	gunpowder	tyre

We give names to these tone-groups according to the tone-pattern heard on the stem of the word (the part of the word after the prefix):

1	2	3	4
rising stem	high stem	falling stem	variable stem

The last group is called the variable stem tone-group because words in this group change their tone-pattern according to the words following, for instance:

naashíta icísóté mwíshitóóló	I bought a hat in the shop.
naashíta icisote cáámúténgó u'úsumá	I bought a cheap hat.

The second tone-pattern is heard when the noun is restricted by an adjective,

15

possessive or participle, which will have the short form of the prefix, or by a relative clause.

In a complete grammar of iciBemba we should have to explain what happens to nouns of each tone-group in the different stable and unstable forms e.g.:

múúpení   it's a knife

nshíkwété mupení   I haven't got a knife

and with the different locative and possessive pre-prefixes e.g.:

kúmupení   with a knife

umútengo wámúpení   the price of the knife.

We should also have to explain the tone-patterns of:

longer nouns like *ulúfungúlo*, 'key',

nouns with a one-syllable prefix like *í-layá*, 'shirt' or *ín-deléshi*, 'dress',

or with a stem beginning in a vowel like *úmw-aná*, 'son or daughter', *úmw-aícé*, 'child',

and nouns with no prefix like *kolwé*, 'monkey'

or with one of the special subsidiary prefixes such as *baa-, cii-* or *kaa-* like *baa-kolwé*, 'monkeys', *kaa-kolwé*, 'little monkey'.

Table 1 (see page 48) gives some of this information, although a lot more explanation and detail would be necessary in a complete grammar. (The table refers to 'tone-sets' rather than 'tone-groups' because the different examples in each set have tone patterns that are similar but not exactly the same).

NOUNS

We have said that every noun in iciBemba belongs to a class. In this outline we have used the word class in the sense of agreement-class, so that *umú-ntú*, 'person', is in one class, while the plural *abá-ntú*, 'people' is in another. There are eighteen of these agreement-classes in iciBemba, fifteen noun-classes and three locative classes which we will explain later. Readers who know Van Sambeek's *A Bemba Grammar* (or many other grammars of Bantu languages) will be used to another sense of class according to which *umú-ntú* and *abá-ntú* are included in the same class with different singular and plural forms. We will refer to a class in this sense as a class-pair or gender. According to Van

16

Sambeek there are nine of these genders in iciBemba, but the number is different in some other grammars.

Here are some nouns in iciBemba with the class-pair numbers they are given by Van Sambeek, and the agreement-class numbers that we use in this outline:

Class-pair Agreement-class

1	1/2	*umúntú/abántú*	person
2	3/4	*úmuti/ímiti*	tree
3	9/10	*ímbushi/ímbushi*	goat
4	7/8	*icítelé/ifítelé*	hen-house, dove-cote
5	5/6	*ífupa/ámafúpá*	bone
6	12/13	*akánwá/utunwá*	mouth
7	11/10	*úlukómbo/ín!kómbo*	drinking vessel
-	11/6	*ulúkásá/amákásá*	foot, footprint
-	14/6	*úbutándá/ámatándá*	mat
8	15/6	*úkubókó/ámabókó*	arm
9	16,17,18	*pá ŋŋandá, kú ŋŋandá, mu ŋŋandá*	at, by or in the house

Nouns in the class-pair 1/2 (class 1 in Van Sambeek), like *umúntú/abántú*, always refer to persons, although some words for person are in other class-pairs, e.g. *íshilu/ámashílú*, 'madman' in 5/6, *ímfumu/ímfumu*, 'chief' in 9/10. Otherwise words with a similar meaning often belong to the same class-pair (for instance *imbwílí/imbwílí*, 'leopard' and other animals in 9/10, *umúpéélá/ imípéélá*, 'guava tree' and other trees in 3/4, with their fruit *ipéélá/ámápéélá* in 5/6) but this does not mean that we can think of animal, tree and fruit as part of the meaning of these class-pairs, nor is the correlation frequent enough to afford any useful rules to someone learning the language.

Nouns have different forms according to their job in the sentence, as we have explained; the different forms of the noun-prefixes in each class in the various forms are given in Table 2 (see page 50).

There are some nouns in iciBemba that have no prefix, although they still have

17

other words agreeing with them, usually as is the case in rural iciBemba with the same agreement as class 1. For instance, we say

úmulúméndo 'ulyá 'that young man',

but *fúndi ulyá* 'that hunter'.

Úmu-lúméndo has a prefix, *fúndi* has not, but both have the adjective prefix *u-* agreeing with them.

The plural of *fúndi* is *baafúndi* 'hunters': *baafúndi balyá* 'those hunters'.

Baafúndi has a prefix, but it is not the same as the ordinary noun prefix in *ába-lúméndo* 'young men'. Nouns like *fundi* are said to belong to the **subsidiary series**. They do not all refer to persons, for instance, we have

fwaka 'tobacco'

kalundwé 'cassava'

and many words from English, like *pénsulo*, 'pencil',
móótoka, 'motor-vehicle'.

In town iciBemba nouns often have different agreements and different plural forms. For the tone-patterns of these nouns, see the lower sections of Table 1.

Sometimes, in addition to their usual prefix, nouns have an extra prefix added to modify their meaning. Less frequently, the new prefix is used in place of the ordinary prefix. Other words have to agree with the added prefix. For instance:

úmu-tóndó wándí náaútobéká	my water-jar is broken
aká-mu-tóndó kándí náakátobéká	my little water-jar is broken
(also: áka-tóndó kándí náakátobéká	my favourite water-jar is broken).

Nouns that normally have no prefix (nouns of the subsidiary series) have special subsidiary prefixes to mark these meanings. For instance:

pénsulo wándí náafúníká	my pencil is broken
kaa- pénsulo kándí náakáfuníká	my little pencil is broken.

Some of the special meanings of these added prefixes are:

specially small or humble things or people : classes 12 and 13 (*aka-/utu-* or *kaa-/tuu-*). Class 13 is plural, and is also used for substances like flour and water that cannot be counted, e.g. *akámúntú* 'dwarf' *utúmenshí* 'a little water'.

Specially large things or people: classes 7 and 8 (*ici-/ifi-* or *cii-/fii-*). Class 8 is plural, and is also used for substances like flour and water, e.g. *ciimóótoka*, 'large vehicle', *ifímaalwá*, 'large quantities of beer'.

Something or someone hopelessly large or clumsy: class 5 (*ili-* - not *i-* in this special sense – or *lii-*). E.g. *ilímúntú*, 'hulking brute'.

Abstract qualities or roles: class 14 (*ubu-* or *buu-*) e.g. *úbufúmú*, 'chieftainship' from *ímfumu*, 'chief', *buukafúndishá*, 'position as teacher' from *kafúndishá*, 'teacher'.

Note that the special use of these classes for things that are specially large or small does not mean that nouns that are normally in these classes are particularly large or small; for instance, *akanwa* is the normal word for mouth and *icikumbi* for eyelid.

ADJECTIVES AND DEMONSTRATIVES

There are relatively few adjectives in iciBemba. The job done by adjectives in English sentences is usually done by participles in iciBemba, or sometimes by nouns with a possessive pre-prefix (as in the examples *úwaíshíbíkwá, ú! wáfyumá* given on page 12).

There are two kinds of adjectives in iciBemba.

Some, like *–sumá* (*umú-sumá*, etc.) - 'good' - may have a prefix of two syllables;

others, like *–mbí* (*'ú-mbí*, etc.) - 'other' - never have a two-syllable prefix.

Adjectives like *–sumá* behave in many ways like nouns. They have stable forms and full and short unstable forms, and they fit into the same tone-sets as nouns. Their prefixes are often like noun-prefixes, but different in one or two classes (see Table 2.) Here are some examples of adjectives like *sumá*:

-bí	bad,
-kalambá or *-kúlú*	big,
-cé	small,
-pya	new,
-káli	fierce, angry.

Adjectives like *mbí* have one unstable form (see Table 2.) The prefix always has a high tone except before *–lyá*, 'that'.

The ordinary stable form is formed by putting *ni-* in front e.g. *niulyá*, 'it's that fellow'.

But some adjectives have a special stable form more like that of the nouns which they use, for instance, after *nangu, nangu 'úúmó*, 'not even one'. Other adjectives of this kind include:-

-ónsé	every, all,
-éná	them,
-ená	as for (the person or thing mentioned),
-nga	how many?,
-éka	alone, by oneself

and the numbers up to five (*-mó, -bílí, -tátú, -ne, -sááno*). The higher numbers are really nouns. (see page 27.)

There are four demonstratives in iciBemba. Two of them are adjectives like *-mbí*:

-nó	this (right by the speaker),
-lyá	that (at a distance from both speaker and listener)

The other two are special forms given in Table 2:

uyú, abá etc.	this (relatively near the speaker),
uyó, abó, etc.	that (relatively near the listener).

Adjectives and demonstratives (and also participles, possessives and relative clauses) are sometimes used without any particular noun to agree with. For instance:

balyá báákali	those (people) are quick-tempered
úwamwéfú nááisá	the bearded man (person of beard) has come
icí cínshi?	what is this?

Classes 1 and 2 are used for persons, classes 7 and 8 for things. Class 14 is used in the same way for abstract things, e.g. *ubútúntúlú*, 'health', from

-*tuntulu*, 'healthy, sound', *umúku wábútátú*, 'the third time, literally time of threeness'.

PERSONAL PRONOUNS AND THE PERSONAL PRE-PREFIX

IciBemba does not normally use a separate personal pronoun to express I, we or you. For instance;

> 'we eat millet' is translated into iciBemba *tulyá ámale*, where 'we' is expressed by the form of the verb.

IciBemba only uses personal pronouns like *ífwé*, 'we', if it wants to contrast two sets of people, for instance;

> *ífwé tulyá ámale, leeló ímwé níkálundwéfye*   we eat millet, but you just eat cassava,

or if it wants to say more exactly who is meant by the pronoun, for instance:

> *fwé baanákáshí tatúlyá ámani*   we women don't eat eggs

There are three forms of the personal pronoun:

> the full form   (like *ífwé*),
>
> the stable form   (like *nifwé*)
>
> the personal pre-prefix   (like *fwé* that can be put before the short form of any nominal or participle:

FULL FORM	STABLE FORM	PERSONAL PREFIX	
íné	*niné*	*né*	I
ífwé	*nifwé*	*fwé*	we
íwé	*niwé*	*wé*	you (familiar)
ímwé	*nimwé*	*mwé*	you (plural or respectful)

There is no third person pronoun for he or they although these words may sometimes be translated by the adjectives –*éná* and *ená*.

21

THE LOCATIVE PRE-PREFIX AND THE LOCATIVE CLASSES

Another kind of pre-prefix that may be added to nominals is called the locative pre-prefix, because it often indicates place.

KúLúsáká	to Lusaka,	}
pákatí	in the middle	} all begin with a locative pre-prefix.
múlibemba	in the lake	}

As well as place, these pre-prefixes often refer to time or to various other special ideas, for instance:

kúntanshi   in the future,

kúbapuupú   by thieves.

There are three different locative classes, each with its own pre-prefix:

Class 17 (*ku-*):	place or time in a general way; person by whom something is done.
Class 16 (*pa-*):	exact place on or at; exact time, as e.g. *pákiifiká* 'immediately on arriving'; cause, e.g. *pámulandú uyó* 'for that reason'.
Class 18 (*mu-*):	place within or along e.g. *mwi!táduni* 'in the township', *múmiisébó* 'along the road', in the course of, e.g. *múkulela úmwaná* 'while looking after the child', *múlicítátú* 'on Wednesday'

The locative classes may mean either 'from', 'to' or 'at' a place, depending on the verb, for instance:

úkúfúma kúLúsáká	to come from Lusaka
ukúya kúLúsáká	to go to Lusaka
ukwíkala kúLúsáká	to live in Lusaka.

The locative pre-prefixes are added to the short form of most kinds of nominal, for instance:

nouns such as *kú-ci-shíma* 'at the well', *mu-ŋ-ŋanda* 'in the house'

adjectives such as *ku-'u-tali* 'from the tall one'.

Nominals that do not have a distinct short form such as demonstratives, adjectives like –*mbi* and the subsidiary classes of nouns, have the special pre-prefixes *páli-*, *kúli-* and *múli-*:

múliúyú múshí	in this village,
(ifísumá) pálifyónsé	(finer) than all,
múlibemba	in the lake.

All words with locative pre-prefixes have stable forms beginning with *ni-, e-* and *tee-*. The tone-patterns of some nouns with locative pre-prefix are shown in Table 1.

Verbs, adjectives and similar kinds of words may agree with the locative pre-prefix, for instance;-

pácishikí pa-lyá	there on the stump,
mwí!óófeshi mw-álíkábá	in the office is hot

Alternatively, such words often have their prefix in one of the locative classes without any noun to agree with for instance:-

palya	there
mwálíkábá	it is hot
ápataléélé (participle)	somewhere cool,
úkutáli (adjective)	somewhere distant
úmwakúséndámá (possessive)	somewhere to sleep.

There are two special forms of the locative pre-prefix;

kúnó- (pánó-, múno-),which has the meaning - here in, etc. - e.g. *kúnó-Lúsáká* 'here in Lusaka',

and *kwá- (páá-, mwá-)*, which is followed by the name (or description) of someone, and refers to their home or village, e.g. *mwáMwamba* 'in Mwamba's village'.

(As many villages are identified by the title of their chief or headman, this is a common way of referring to places.)

There is a set of personal stems used only with the locative pre-prefixes:

-mwandí	'my home or village' e.g. *múmwandí* 'in my village', *kúnó-mwandí* 'here at my house'
-mwesú	our home,

-*moobé*	your home (familiar),
-*mwenú*	your home (plural or polite),
-*mwakwé*	his home,
-*mwabó*	their home.

THE POSSESSIVE PREFIX AND THE POSSESSIVE PRONOUN

The phrase *iŋŋandá yá-mulúméndo*, 'the young man's house', shows another kind of pre-prefix which is often translated in English by 'of' or the possessive 's. There is a separate pre-prefix for every class (see the list in Table 2) and the pre-prefix has to agree like an adjective with the word it is modifying (the pre-prefix *yá-* is in class 9 agreeing with *iŋ-ŋandá*).

This possessive pre-prefix has many other functions besides indicating owners; for instance:-

it can indicate a quality, e.g. *umúshi wábúsáká*	a tidy village (village of tidiness)
or contents, e.g. *icípe cáábwálí*	a plate of nshima (cereal),

and it is often used with the infinitive in expressions like *ámenshí yákunwá* 'drinking water', *umúpika wákwípikilamó úmunani* 'a saucepan for cooking relish in'.

Like adjectives, it can be used without any particular noun to agree with, for instance:-

ábaa-múcinshí	respectful people (people of respect),
icaa-fyé	something trivial (from 'it of no consequence').

The possessive pre-prefix has both full and short unstable forms, as well as stable forms beginning *e-* and *tee-*. It is added to the short form of any nominal, except that before a noun with no prefix in dictating a particular person or animal, the element *–kwa-* is put in between, e.g.

ubúkula bwákwaMwamba, 'Mwamba's cultivation', but *ubúkula bwámfumu*, 'the chief's cultivation', because *mfumu* has a prefix.

ímpapa yákwákolwé, 'the monkey's skin', but *impapa yákolwé*, 'monkey skin'.

24

Pre-prefixes of different kinds can be added to one another, e.g.

úbwalwá bwá-mú-mbékétí   the beer (of) in the bucket,

or even ícaamúlwápálúkungú   the one (e.g. icípushí 'pumpkin') in the one (e.g. ulúpé 'basket') on the verandah.

If we don't need to repeat the owner (or other idea expressed by the possessive pre-prefix) we can use a possessive pronoun, for instance:-

ísabi lyáfúmá múbwendo bwálíko   the fish has come out of its hole,

í!téébulo nénsalú yápáko   the table and its cloth (the cloth of on it)

The pronoun *(bwálíko* and *yápáko)* has a pre-prefix agreeing with the modified noun *(ubwéndó* and *ínsalú)*, but the stem of the pronoun agrees with the word it is standing for, *liko* with *ísabi*, 'fish' and *-páko* with the locative *péé!téébulo*, 'on the table'.

There are also personal possessive pronouns such as *-andí*, 'my', *-enú*, 'your' (see Table 3).

Na- 'and, with', *nga-* 'like'

Two elements come even before the pre-prefixes and are often incorrectly written as separate words:

na-, which is often translated 'and, also, even, with'

and *nga-*, often translated 'like'. Here are some examples:

ábaaúmé náábaanákáshí	men and women
bááíkálá báásámba nakúminwe	they sat down **and washed their hands**
naíwé winé tuléékuuma	we shall beat even you
twaísa nabááShímusenge	we came with Shimusenge
bálí neemílímó	they have work (literally ...are with... -this construction commonly translates English have)

múpeepí nakwísano ukwénsha (móotoka)	near the chief's court
ngééshilu	to drive like a madman

Note that when *na-* joins clauses, it is added to the first nominal in the clause *(kúminwe* in the sentence above) and not to the verb.

There are special pronouns (listed in Table 3) which may stand in the place of nominals beginning with *na-*, for instance:

bááítá Canda, naó áákaana ati ˈnshínwá	they invited Chanda, and he declined saying "I don't drink".
twaisa naabó	we came with him (them)
'múpeepí nakó	near there.

There are different forms of this pronoun for class 1 and 2 and I, we and you;
> one is used roughly for the constructions in which *na-* might be translated 'and', 'also' or 'even',
> the other for constructions in which *na-* might be translated 'with'.

NOMINAL PHRASES

We have noticed that various kinds of nominal may take the place of a noun in a sentence. For instance, instead of *úmulúnshí nááisá* 'the hunter has come', we may say *úmutálí* or *uyú* or *úwamfúti nááisá* 'the tall one' or 'this one' or 'the one with the gun' has come.

The noun can also be expanded into a nominal phrase, for instance:

inshíta 'ikalamba	a long time
í!túmba lyápácifuba	breast pocket
i 'í misango twátóólá	these habits we've picked up
fwé-bashíkwêté ncinga	we who haven't any bicycles.

Qualifying words (like adjectives and participles) normally follow the head-word of the phrase (*inshíta, i!túmba, misango* and *fwé-* in these examples) but demonstratives (like *i!i*) may be placed in front or following. The last two examples are types of relative clause, discussed more fully in Chapter 5.

26

Numbers up to five are adjectives, and follow the words they agree with. Numbers over five also follow, but these numbers are really nouns, and do not agree with what precedes. For instance:

inkoko mutanda	six hens
inkoko ikumi (límó)	ten hens

Límó is the adjective 'one' agreeing with *íkumi* 'ten'. Eleven would be *íkumi naímó,* where *ímó* agrees with *ínkoko.* Similarly for twenty:

Ínkoko ámakúmí yábílí	twenty hens

where *yábílí* is an adjective agreeing with *ámakúmí* 'tens'. This is similar to the way of giving weights and measures:

ubúngá í!paundi límó	one lb. flour
ubúngá ámapááundi yábílí	two lbs. flour.

These numbers are often replaced by Bemba forms of English numbers, e.g. *wáánu, túu, filíi.*

Ordinal numbers (first, second, third etc.) are shown in one of two ways:

úbushikú bwácíne (or bwábúne)	the fourth day (day of fourness)
úbushikú bwalengá shíne	the fourth day (the day bringing the total to four days. *Shíne* agrees with *ínshiku* days).

Chapter 3
VERBS

This chapter covers

finite verb-forms like *báalífyúká,* 'they have escaped' or *twénde,* 'let us go',

imperatives like *njafwééníko,* 'help me',

infinitives like *úkulómbá,* 'to beg' or *úkuláashífwáya,* 'to keep looking for them'

and participles like *ábeekalamó,* 'those who live there', *éwatúpúswíshé,* 'it was he who rescued us'.

PRONOUNS

Every finite verb-form has a pronoun prefix that agrees with or stands for the subject of the verb (the person or thing that the clause is about) e.g.:

-ba- 'they' in *bá-alífyúká,*

tw- 'we' in *tw-énde,*

ákaaíce ká-léélilá, 'the child is crying',

kúnó kw-átálálá 'it is chilly here'.

Participles have a similar prefix, for example

ilúba ly-akáshíká 'the red flower', which agrees like an adjective with the word the participle is modifying or standing for.

The participle prefix has full and short stable forms as well as stable forms beginning *e-* and *tee-*.

All verb-forms, including the infinitive, may have a pronoun representing the direct object, for instance:-

nj- 'me' in *nj-afwééníko*

-shí- 'them' referring, for instance, to *ímbushi* 'goats' in *úkuláashífwáya.*

These object pronouns always come immediately before the verb-root.

Not all objects are direct objects; for instance in

naapééla úmwaícé icítábó 'I gave a book to the child', *umwaice,* 'child' is direct object, and can be represented by an object pronoun in the verb: *náámupééla icítábó* 'I gave him a book'. But we cannot represent *icítábó* 'book' by a pronoun in the verb, as it is an indirect object. Notice that in English grammar, book is the direct object, and child the indirect object.

Differences like this often occur between languages, and easily lead to mistakes. Neither is more correct than the other; it simply means that we must study a foreign language as it is, and not guess at what it is like from the languages we know.

The last kind of pronoun has the form

-po (Class 16),

-*ko* (Class 17),

and -*mo* (Class 18),

and can occur at the very end of a verb-form, for instance

ábeekalamó (those who live there).

This pronoun often refers to place in the same way as other forms in the locative classes, but it has a number of other uses which are more difficult to define. If the tone before the pronoun is high, the tone on the pronoun slips and is heard as low.

The subject and object pronouns and the participle prefix are listed in Table 3.

TENSE-SIGNS

A **finite** verb form contains, besides the **root**, such as -*fik*-, 'arrive' and –*fúm*- 'come from' and the pronouns we have just described, one or more parts which together serve to indicate what we call the tense of the verb, i.e. when the action happens, whether it is still going on and so on. For instance, using the pronoun *tu*- *tw*- 'we' and the root -*fik*- 'arrive', we may say:

tw-a – fik-ílé	we arrived (some days ago)
tw-a – fík-á	we have just arrived
tu-ka – fik-a	we will arrive
tu-léé – fik-á	we are arriving
náa-tú – fik-á	we have arrived.

There is always one of these tense-signs at the end, after the root but before -*pó*, -*kó* or -*mó*, except in the case of the irregular verbs 'to be' and 'to say'.

In many tenses, but not all, there is another tense-sign before the root- -*a*-, -*ka*- and –*léé*-.

In these examples; if there is an object pronoun as well, the tense-sign comes first, e.g.

tu-ka-bá-shíndík-á   we will accompany them.

A few tenses have a tense-sign before the subject pronoun, like the *náa*- in *náatúfiká*. In the tables of tenses (pp 54 and 56), the place of each of the tense-signs is shown by the examples, and also by the use of hyphens.

The last tense-sign in *twafikílé*, 'we arrived', has a number of different forms. For instance, these words are all in the same tense:

twafúm-íné	we left
twaend-élé	we travelled
twakós-éshé	we lit (a fire).

The ending is;

-*ine* (or -*ene*) instead of *ile* (or -*ele*) if the root ends in *m, n, ŋ,* or *ny*,

–*ele* (or -*ene*) instead of –*ile* (or –*ine*) if the previous vowel is *e;*

–*eshe* (or *ishe*) when the root normally ends in *y* or *sh* (notice the way the root ends in *twakósh-á umúlilo*, 'we have just lit a fire'.

Endings are even more complicated with longer roots (and a few irregular short roots like –*món-)*:

twashíndííké	we accompanied	— compare *twashíndíka*
twaikéélé	we stayed	— compare *twaíkala*
twamwéné	we saw	— compare *twamóná;*

It is as if –*i*- is put in just before the end of the root: *shindi (-i-)k-e, -ika(-i-)l-e, -mo(-i-)n-e*. The form that this ending takes with each verb is shown in the *White Fathers' Bemba-English Dictionary*; they have spelt the ending –*lLe* with capital letters to show the ending takes many other forms.

Negative ('not') tenses usually start with *ta-:* but 'relative' tenses and participles have –*shi*- instead put immediately after the subject pronoun. *Shi*- is also used instead of *ta*- after *n*- (I), e.g.

shí-leefwáya	I don't want,
but *ta-tú-leefwáya*	we don't want.

Negative tenses are often quite different from the corresponding affirmative tenses, as can be seen from Table 4a. The subjunctive tenses use a special sign –*i*- to mark the negative, for instance *tu-i-y-á* 'let us not go'.

TONE-PATTERNS IN THE VERB-FORM

All the pronouns and tense-signs we have mentioned in the previous two chapters, as well as the root and certain other features to be mentioned in the next chapter, can affect the tone-pattern of a verb-form. Compare, for example, *náabá-bómb-á* 'they have worked hard' and *náabá-bómb-á* 'they have got wet'. The root *-bómb-* and the root *-bomb-* are different words with quite different meanings. The infinitive *úku-bómb-á* 'to work hard' has a tone-pattern like that of nouns with high stem-tone; the infinitive *ukú-bómb-á* 'to get wet' has a tone-pattern like nouns with variable stem-tone. Here are some other examples where the tone-pattern changes because of the tone-set of the verb-root:

báafúndílé ábaaná	they taught the children
bááfundílé ímpombó	they skinned the duiker
ukúshiika ícaalá	to bury a corpse
úkushííka úbwató	to paddle a boat

Subject and object pronouns do not all have the same tone as one another (see Table 3). Compare, for example:

tuléémutúká ínselé	we are insulting him
tuléemútúká ínselé	we are insulting you
útwaícé túléémutúká ínselé	the children are insulting him
útwaícé túleemútúká ínselé	the children are insulting you.

It is tone that enables us to tell the difference between 'him' and 'you' and between 'we' and Class 13, (*tu* standing for *utwaice*)

Tone also sometimes serves to distinguish tenses that are otherwise identical. For instance:

twafíkile (mailo) kúmwesú	we got home yesterday
twafikílé kalé kúmwesú	we got home some days ago
tuléelyá ubwálí	we are eating nshima.
túleelyá ubwálí	should we eat nshima?

In Table 4a we have given two examples of each tense;
the first example uses a verb like *ukú-bílá* 'to sew', which has the variable stem tone-pattern;
the second example uses a verb like *úku-cápá* 'to wash', which has the high stem tone-pattern.

31

We have not marked any tones on the tense-signs printed above each pair of examples because the tones actually heard on each part of the word often vary, for instance:

bá-ká-bil-a kaputúla	they will sew a pair of shorts
bá-ka-cáp-á kaputúla	they will wash a pair of shorts.

Although the tone-patterns may at first seem very complicated, they are in fact quite regular, although it is not practicable in this outline to explain all the rules involved. The tones that are actually heard depend on the essential tones of each part of the verb, which may be determined or neutral. For instance, in *bákábila and bákacápá, ba-* and *–cap-* are both determined, the other parts are all neutral.

A determined syllable normally becomes high, and makes the next syllable high as well, unless there is only one neutral syllable between two determined syllables. So:-

-*ká-* in *bákábila* is made high by *bá-*,

-*á* in *bákacápá* is made high by *ba-*,

-*a* in *bakacapa* is made high by *–cáp-*,

but -*ka-* is not high in *bákacápá* because there is only one neutral syllable between *bá-* and *–cáp-*.

These essential tones are very like the ones described in the Tonga outline, but the rules explaining the tones actually heard are very different.

A special kind of tone-pattern called **diatony** is used in a number of tenses. In this pattern, all the syllables after the last determined syllable become high, for instance

bálábílá	they sew (where *ba-* is determined),
bálacápá	they wash (where *bá-* and *–cáp-* are both determined).

INDICATIVE TENSES

There are two sets of indicative tenses in iciBemba,

the bound set, used when attention is centred on the object,

and the unbound set, when attention is centred on the verb itself.

(They are similar to the weak and strong tenses in ciTonga.) For instance

| *tulapeepa* | 'we smoke (or take snuff)' uses an unbound tense, |
| while *tupeepa úwamúmyóná* | 'we take snuff' uses the bound tense because the interest is centred on the object. |

The unbound tenses sometimes have different tense-signs, as here, but often the difference is only one of tone, the unbound tenses displaying diatony, for instance:-

| *bákábila kaputúla* | they will sew the shorts, |
| *bákábílá* | they will sew. |

For each pair of bound and unbound tenses there is also a relative tense and a participle, based in form on the bound tense. For instance:

Eo tupeepa 'that's the kind (of tobacco or snuff) we take' is an example with a relative tense;

ábapeepa úwamúnyóná báánakashi nábaaúmé bakalambá 'those who take snuff are women and old men' begins with a participle.

Each has a characteristic tone-pattern. In the relative tenses the first and last tones are normally raised, although the last syllable may sometimes be a slipped high heard as low, as in *túpéépa*. In the participle, the first two tones (in the full form) are always high-low.

Table 4a gives some of the principal bound tenses describing actions that simply happen and actions that go on for a time. It will be noticed that iciBemba divides time up much more exactly than English tenses into earlier today, yesterday, some days ago and so on.

These translations are only a guide to the way the tenses are used; the 'yesterday' tense may equally refer to 'last week', 'last month', 'last year', and the 'some days ago' tense to any time before that. In telling stories or relating incidents, the time is indicated by the tense used in the first sentence, and then things that happened afterwards are described using the *–a-'- -a* 'just now' tense, or the *–alaa'- -a* 'shortly' tense if they go on for a time.

PERFECT AND HABITUAL TENSES

Table 4b gives **perfect tenses** (describing how things are naturally or as a result of actions) and **habitual tenses** (describing things that happen regularly).

There are a large number of verb-roots in iciBemba which regularly occur in one of these perfect tenses, while the equivalent ideas in English are stressed by a simple present, for instance

nínjíshíbá	I know,
báalíkúlá	they are grown up.

This leads to mistakes in English such as 'I am knowing' and mistakes in iciBemba such as *ndéeíshíbá*. It may help to think of the basic meaning of these words as 'to get to know', 'to become grown up' and so on.

HYPOTHETICAL TENSES

The table below gives the tenses used in sentences like *abálábá úmucele, nga tatwákwété caakúlungilakó innámá*, 'if they had forgotten the salt, we wouldn't have had anything to season the meat with', where the clause beginning 'if...' refers to something that didn't actually happen, but is only imagined. They are not used in sentences like *nga aalábá úmucele, tatwakwáté cáákúlungilakó innámá* 'if he forgets the salt, we won't have anything to season the meat with', where the 'if...' clause refers to something that may happen. In the second type of sentence, *nga* is used in the 'if...' clause; in the first type of sentence *nga* is used in a clause that describes the consequences.

HYPOTHETICAL TENSES

Simple actions	Continuous actions
a- -a	*a- -laa'- -a*
abálubá if they had got lost	*abálááluba* if they had kept getting lost
abálábá if they had forgotten	*abáláalábá* if they had kept forgetting

34

SUBJUNCTIVE TENSES AND THE IMPERATIVE

The imperative form of a verb is used for giving orders or instructions. For instance, we might say to a child

isá kúnó	come here
or *búúla*	take this.

This form is made from the verb-root and the suffix *-a*

If an object pronoun is added, the suffixal ending changes to *-e*. For instance:

bá-twálil-é	take it to them.

Politer forms are made by adding *-iní*

isééni kúnó,	*(isa + - ini)*
búúleení	*(buula + - ini)*
bátwálilééni	*(batwalile + - ini)*

The first *i* of *-iní* runs together with the *-a* or *-e* at the end for the more familiar forms to give *-eení*.

The imperative is only used for orders that are to be carried out immediately; otherwise the subjunctive is used. For instance

endééní kwishitoolo, múnshitiléko fwaka	go to the shop and buy me some tobacco,
múkeesé páliCítátú	come on Wednesday.

The subjunctive is similarly used for orders not to do something:

mwicítá ícongó	don't make noise.

The imperative and subjunctive may have in front of them one of the special prefixes

áku-	invitation,
shí-	asserting authority,
naa-	polite suggestion
or *ka-*	go and...

For instance:

naatúleeyá	shall we be off?
ákulyééni	don't wait, start eating,

35

| *shípítééní apá* | come this way, |
| *kánje-búúla akálímbá* | let me go and get my radio. |

The subjunctive has a number of other uses, some of which will be referred to in Chapter 5.

SUBJUNCTIVE TENSES

-e	*-ka- -e*	*-lee' -a*	*-kalee' -a*
should they sew		should they get sewing	
bábilé	*bákabilé*	*báleebíla*	*bákaléébila*
should they wash		should they get washing	
bácapé	*bákacápé*	*báleecápá*	*bàkaléecápá*
Negative			
-i- -a	*-ika- -a*	*-ilaa' -a*	*-ikalaa'- -a*
shouldn't they sew		shouldn't they keep sewing	
béébilá	*béékabilá*	*bééláábila*	*béékaléébila*
shouldn't they wash		shouldn't they keep washing	
béécápá	*béékacápá*	*bééláacápá*	*béékaláacápá*

INFINITIVE

Examples of infinitives are

úkwangálá	to amuse oneself,
úkubááfwáko	to help them with it
úkuláabómbá	to work continually,

They all begin with the prefix *uku-* which is like a noun prefix in Class 15. It has short and stable forms and can have words agreeing with it, for instance:

| *úkubéyá umúshíshí kútálúsha índa* | cutting the hair keeps lice away |
| *kúúícúúshafyé* | it is to put oneself to pains for nothing. |

As well as the object pronoun and *–pó, -kó* and *-mó* (as in *úkubááfwáko*), the infinitive can have the tense-sign *-láa-* (as in *úkuláabómbá*) to mark continuity.

'To Be' and 'To Say'

The verb *úkubá* 'to be or to become' is only used in tenses that end *–a* or *–e*. In tenses that normally end *-ILe* the special root *–li* is used, without any tense-sign at the end. For instance:

áabá noomúcinshí	he is (naturally) polite	(*-a'- -a* 'perfect tense)
alí nensála	he is hungry (at the moment)	(ILe perfect tense).

The verb *ukútiila* 'to say' has another form ending *–ti*, which is used to form some tenses without any tense-ending. One such tense is equivalent to the *–a'- -a* just now tense, e.g.

    bááti   they said.

Another is unlike any ordinary tense in form, and it has the special job of introducing reported speech, e.g.

báámwéba abáti...	they told him that...,
ááy'asuka ati...	he answered that....

Although this verb is often translated 'to say,' it has a number of other uses. It may be used with certain tenses of other verbs to yield a compound tense, e.g. *báátí básosé ifí* 'just as he said this'. It is also used in a special type of noun phrase described in Chapter 5.

DERIVED FORMS OF THE VERB ROOT

So far we have talked about the verb-root as if it was never made up of more than one part. In fact iciBemba, like most Bantu languages, has many longer roots built up from shorter ones by suffixes or extensions which modify the meaning. For instance:

-lémb-,	write,
-lémb-el-	write to,
-lémb-w-	be written,
-lémb-esh-	cause to write.

This section describes some of the most important of these extensions.

One of the commonest extensions, often called the **applicative extension**, introduces someone affected by the action, for instance:

alééipika úmunani	she is cooking relish
alééipikila abééní úmunani	she is cooking relish for the guests
bááíbá ínkoko	they have stolen a hen
báánjíbíla ínkoko	they have stolen my hen.

When this extension is used, the person affected is treated as the direct object, and can be represented by the object pronoun, but the original object cannot, so that

we can say *aléebéépikila úmunani*	she is cooking them the relish,
but not *aléewípikila abééni*	she is cooking it for the guests.

The extension sometimes takes the form *–el-*, *-in-* or *en-* and occasionally other forms. Rather like the tense-sign we wrote *ll.e.* so we will write this extension *–IL-* to show it takes these different forms.

The *-IL-* extension has a number of other uses. It can be used with a locative to show that the meaning is towards or at rather than away from, for instance:

ísabi lyáfúmá múmenshí	the fish has come out of the water,
lyáfúmína kúnse	it has come out onto the surface.

It can be used to give a reason, for instance:

aléélenganshí? 'what is he drawing', becomes *aléélengelanshí icíkópé?* 'what is he drawing the picture for?'.

Lastly it introduces the thing used to perform an action with, for instance:

úkupútúla umwándó	to cut a rope,
úkupútwíla umwándó kumwele	to cut the rope with a knife,
ukúsenda úbuubá	to carry fish-poison,
ukúsendela múmíséké	to carry it in baskets.

The **causative extension** introduces the person responsible for an action in some way, for instance:

ábalúméndo báákáka ifípé	the young men have tied up the loads

kapitáo áábákákisha ifípé	the foreman made them tie up the loads
kapitáo aakákisha ifípé	the foreman had the loads tied up
aafikákisha	he had them tied up.

It will be seen that either the original subject, here *ábalúméndo* 'young men' or the original object, here *ifípé* 'loads' can be treated as direct object, but not both.

The extension sometimes has the form *–ish–* or *–esh–*, as here; sometimes *–ik–* (*-ek-*), but most commonly the last consonant of the root is changed to *sh* or *fy*, or *y* is added, e.g.:-

-lub-	get lost	*-lufy-*	lose
-lil-	cry	*-lish-*	cause to cry
-onk-	suck	*-onsh-*	suckle, give suck
-fum-	come out	*-fumy-*	make...come out, get out.

There are two extensions that may seem alike to English-speakers, as both are translated by the English passive voice. For instance: *-tob-ek-* and *–tob-w-* can both be translated 'be smashed'.

The first of these is especially used in the perfect tenses to describe a state, for instance *úmutóndó wálitóbéká* 'the pot is broken', and so it is called the **stative extension**.

The second is used when one is thinking not of the state but the action of someone in causing the state, although the person need not be mentioned and is called the **passive extension.**

| *úmutóndó wátóbwa kúbaaícé* | the pot has been smashed by the children, |
| *úmutóndó wátóbwá* | the pot has been smashed. |

The stative extension has the form *–ik–* (or *–ek–*),
or sometimes *–am–* (e.g. *–petam–* 'be bent'),

The passive extension has the form *–w–* (or *–iw–*). The passive voice is very common in English, and English-speakers speaking iciBemba often use the

39

passive extension more than a Bemba would, for instance, saying *Mulenga náaíkátwá*, 'Mulenga has been arrested', when a Bemba might say *náabéékata Mulenga*, 'they have arrested Mulenga', without mentioning who they are.

There are numerous pairs of **verb-roots**,
one ending *–ul-* (or *–ol-*, *-on-* etc.),
the other ending *–uk-* (or *–ok-*), for instance:

-ipul-	remove (a saucepan or something similar) from the fire,
-ipuk-	is off the fire,
-nukul-	pick (something like mushrooms),
-nukuk-	be picked.

The root ending in *–ul-* appears to be the causative of the root ending in *–uk-*. The root ending in *–uk-* is the stative of the root ending *–ul-*. Here is another example in which the ending *–ul-* is itself an extension with the meaning 'undo something':

-kak- 'tie', *-kakul-* 'untie', *-kakuk-* 'become untied'.

Another extension *-an-* is often translated 'one another', for instance:

-íshiban-	know one another,
-umfwan-	understand one another, get on well together.

The subject pronoun is always plural, and the verb is often followed by *na-* 'with' or the corresponding pronoun:

tuloomfwána nabaaMulenga	I get on well with Mulenga
tuloomfwána naabó	I get on well with him.

There are various other extensions which sometimes alter the meaning of a root. They do not all occur with every root, but the following examples will give an idea of the variety:

-bómb-	work	*-bómbesh-*	work hard
-fw-	die, break down	*-fwilil-*	break down beyond repair
-pend-	count	*-pendulul-*	recount
-lepul-	tear	*-lepaul-*	tear roughly

40

Chapter 4
FURTHER KINDS OF WORDS

Besides verbs and the various kinds of word we have called nominals, there are many words in iciBemba that could be described as adverbs, conjunctions, interjections and so on. We are not going to say much about words of this kind in this outline for two reasons: firstly, these words are not usually built up of separate parts like the prefix and stem of nouns or the many parts of verbs, so we cannot describe their structure; secondly, if we tried to describe the way they fitted into sentences, we would have to treat almost every word separately. That sort of information would be far too long for this outline, and ought to come in a dictionary.

It is in any case not easy to decide what part of speech many Bemba words belong to, for instance

kalé 'long ago' would normally be called an adverb, but it can be used with
the possessive pre-prefix as in *ábáákalé* 'people of long ago' like a noun.

Words often belong to quite different parts of speech in iciBemba and English: 'until' is a conjunction in English, but it is translated by the verb *–suk-:*

| *báálímá báálímá bwásúka bwáila* | they hoed and hoed until it got dark. |

The three forms *–pó, -kó* and *-mó* which we have mentioned occurring at the very end of verb-forms also occur at the end of nominals, e.g.

| *nafímbipo* | and other things as well, |
| *kasalánga nénkókómo* | a cage with a hen in it. |

There are three other forms which we have not mentioned that similarly occur after both verbs and nominals:

| *-fyé* | just, only (the form is very difficult to translate), |
| *-pé* | continually, |

41

-nshí?	what,		
	e.g.	*múúlandúnshi*	for what reason, why?,
		báábwélakófye	they simply came back (implying they were unsuccessful).

These forms are usually written as part of the word before, but in some respects they are more like separate words; they all have high tone if the tone before is low, but low if it is high.

A number of adjectives and pronouns have special adverbial meanings in certain classes. Words of this kind in Class 5 have the special meaning of time or number of times, for instance

lilyá	then,
líbílí	twice.

Words in Class 8 similarly mean the way something is done:

ifî	like this,
ifyo (relative pronoun)	how.

There are one or two words in Class 7 which give the reason for something:

ico (relative pronoun)	because.

There is a group of special words in iciBemba used with the verb *-ti* 'say' or *na-* 'with' to indicate kinds of movement and sound, e.g.

ukúti mpuu	to thud on something

This type of word is called an **ideophone.** Similar words are common in spoken English, though less often in written English, after the verb 'to go':

to go splosh through the puddle,

to go whoomp against the wall.

Another kind of word, also sometimes called an ideophone, is used to strengthen (or intensify) the meaning of particular verbs, and so is called an **intensive**:

úkwisúlá páá	to be brim full,

42

úkukáshíká céé   to be bright red.

Chapter 5
SENTENCES AND THEIR PARTS

Nga aabwélakó, naaláalómbá útwakúsanika mu ɲɲanda, 'When he returns, I will beg a little oil to light the house'.

This sentence has two main parts, or clauses – *Nga aabwélakó* and *naaláalómbá útwakúsanika mu ɲɲanda*, each with its own finite verb (*aabwélakó* and *naaláalómbá*). Part of the second clause, *útwakúsanika mu ɲɲanda*, 'something to light the house', is very like a clause itself, except that it contains the infinitive -*kúsanika*, 'to light' instead of a finite verb like *naaláásanika*, 'I shall light'; but it is doing the job of a noun or noun-phrase like *utúmafútá*, 'a little oil'. This chapter is about a few special kinds of finite clause (like nga *aabwélakó*) and secondary clauses working as phrases (like *útwakúsanika mu ɲɲanda*).

Here is a sentence with the two types of clause we want to consider:
Aapóshá cuufi munánkwe, úwaupílé umúkulambá wámukásháána ulyá áákobékéélé.
'He greeted his brother in-law, the man who had married the elder sister of the girl to whom he had become engaged.'

In the English translation, there are two relative clauses explaining something about a word in the clause before: the clause beginning 'who had married...' (explaining about the brother-in-law), and the clause 'to whom he had became engaged' (explaining about the younger sister). In the Bemba sentence there are two different kinds of clause, one with a participle (*úwaupílé*), the other with a relative tense *áákobékéélé*.

Participle clauses (like *úwaupílé umúkalambá wámukásháána ulyá*) are usually used when the word being explained is the subject of the explanatory clause. (We can confirm this if we see whether the subject pronoun of the verb would

43

agree with the word being explained if we made a separate sentence of the explanation, such as *cuufì munánkwe ááupílé umúkalambá* 'the brother-in-law married the elder sister'- the prefix of *a-aupile* does agree with *cuufì munánkwe.*) The subject of the explanatory clause can be in a locative class, for instance:

> *múŋŋandá musendama imbushi mwâlínúnka*, 'it is smelly in the house where the goats sleep'. In the equivalent sentence, *muŋŋanda ilyá múséndama ímbushi*, 'that house has goats sleeping in it', the prefix of *múséndama* does agree with *muŋŋanda.*

Occasionally participle clauses are used when the word explained is not the subject of the explanatory clause, e.g.

> *ifìsósá ábaanákáshí fyábúwelewele* 'what women say is trivial' – the equivalent sentence *ábaanákáshí básósá ifì nafyakúti* 'women say so-and-so', the prefix of *ba-sosa* does not agree with what is being explained.

Relative clauses, like *áákobékéélé*, 'to whom he was engaged', are used when the word being explained is not the subject of the explanatory clause. *Úmukáshaána ulyá* is object of the equivalent sentence *áákobékéélé úmukásháána ulyá*, 'he got engaged to that girl'. Relative clauses often begin with a special relative pronoun, for instance, we might have said *úmukásháána úo áákobékéélé.*

When the word being explained is neither subject nor object of the explanatory clause, its job in the explanatory clause has to be shown by pronouns. It is easiest to illustrate this by starting with a simple sentence, and then an equivalent relative clause.

Using a *na-* pronoun:

twakúmééné nóómulúméndo munshila	we met a young man on the way
úmulúmendo úo twákúmééné nankwé múnshílá	the young man we met on the way

using a possessive pronoun:

bááfímba íŋŋandá yákwákantwá	they have roofed so-and-

| | so's house |
| úo bááfimba íŋŋandá yákwé | whose house they have roofed |

Using a locative ending to the verb (-po, -ko, -mo):

| tufundila innámá kúmwelé | we skin animals with a knife |
| úmwelé úo túfúndiláko innámá | the knife we skin animals with. |

Both relative and participle clauses are used to make a special kind of sentence which picks out one piece of information in the sentence as of particular interest or importance. For instance:

1)	*Mulenga aatásha ín!cínga yákwáCanda*	Mulenga admired Chanda's bicycle
2)	*NiMulenga éwatásha ín!cínga yákwáCanda*	It was Mulenga who (has just) admired Chanda's bicycle
3)	*Nin!cinga yákwáCanda éyo Mulenga áátásha*	It was Chanda's bicycle that Mulenga admired
4)	*NiCanda, éo Mulenga áátásha in!cinga yákwé*	It was Chanda whose bicycle Mulenga admired.

In each case the word or phrase picked out comes first and is usually put in the stable form.

Sentence (2) picks out the subject *(Mulenga)* and uses a participle clause with the definite stable form of the participle beginning *e-*.

Sentences (3) and (4) use relative clauses with the relative pronoun in the stable form beginning *e-*.

As with ordinary relative clauses, pronouns (like *yákwé*) may be used to show the job the word picked out has in the relative clause.

One type of expression rather like a relative clause uses a clause with infinitive and possessive pre-prefix to explain the purpose or function of something. Here are some examples:

abaakúsunka móótoka	people to push a car
i!fyákufwálá	things to wear, clothes
úlukómbo lwákunwámo ámenshí	a cup to drink water from
úmwelé wákúfundilakó innámá	a knife to skin animals with.

In this case, too, pronouns, like *–mó* and *–kó* in the last two examples, are used to show the job the word being explained does in the infinitive clause.

There is a similar type of expression with *ukúti* and a verb in the subjunctive instead of the infinitive, for instance:

úlukómbo úlwakúti tú'nwemo ámenshí 'a cup for us to drink water from'.

The difference between this and an expression like *úlukómbo lwákunwámo ámenshí* is that it allows us to mention the subject of the infinitive clause (in this case, who it is who wants to drink).

Questions in iciBemba are very similar to ordinary sentences. Those to which the expected answer is 'yes' or 'no' are marked either by *bushé* or simply by raised tones at the end of the sentence, e.g.

bushé mukabwelakó mailo?

or simply *mukabwelakó mailo?*   will you come back tomorrow?.

Other questions may resemble an ordinary sentence with a question word put for what one wants to know, for instance:

Ordinary sentence	*naabííka péé!téébulo*	I put it on the table
Question	*mwabííka píi?*	Where did you put it?

Alternatively, the question word may come first in the stable form, with the verb in a relative tense:

nipíi mwábííka?   Where did you put it?

The question word, *píi* 'where', 'on what' is used when the answer expected is a locative word in Class 16.

There are similar question words for Class 17: *kwî* 'where' and Class 18: *mwî*

46

'where', 'in what'.

If the answer expected is a person 'who', the question word is *áni* or *nááni* (plural *baani*); this word is really a noun, and can have the possessive pre-prefix, for instance;-

    icítabo cáákwáni or *cáábááni*   whose book?

or the special locative-possessive pre-prefix *kwá-* or *páá-* or *mwá-*;

    kwá-áni   at whose house?

'What' is translated by the special form *-nshí* or by *cínshi* (plural *fínshi*), really an adjective like *-mbí-* for instance;-

    bálééfwayanshi?

    or *cínshi bálééfwáyá?*   what do they want?

-nshí can be preceded by the possessive pre-prefix, e.g. *cáánshi?* (of what, what's it made of? or what's it for?).

Here are a few more question words:

    -nga (an adjective like *-mbí*)   how many,

    liiláli   when,

    shááni   how.

TABLE 1 - NOUN TONE-PATTERNS

Tone-Set	Full Form	Short Form	Stable Form (Indefinite)	Forms With Pre-Prefix	Possessive (Full Form)	Possessive (Short Form)	Meaning
Rising stem	ici-pushi	cipushi	ciipushi	múcipushi	icáacipushi	cáácipushi	pumpkin
	in-saká	nsaká	ninsaká	pánsaká	i!cáánsaká	cáánsaká	village meeting-place
	ily-ashi	lyashi	lyáshi	miIyashi	i!cáályashi	cáályashi	conversation
Falling stem	ici-shima	cishima	ci!shima	kúcishima	icáácishima	cáácishima	well
	in-!cito	ncito	nin!cito	kún!cito	icáancito	caánciito	job
	u!bw-áfya	bwáfya	bwáfya	mi!bwáfya	icáabwáfya	caabwáfya	difficulty
High stem	umu-célé	mucélé	miúcele	múmucélé	i!cáamucélé	cáámucélé	salt
	imfumu	mfumu	nimfumu	kúmfumu	i!cáimfumu	caamfúmu	chief
Variable stem (restricted)	umu-shi	mushi or mushi	múúshi	kúmushi	icáamishi	cáámushi	village
(un-restricted)	umi-shi	mushi or mushi	múúshi	kúmishi	icaamishi	cáámishi	village
Subsidiary Class Nouns without Prefix							
Rising Stem		kohwé	nikohwé	kúilikohwé	i!cáákohwé	cáákohwé	monkey
Falling or high stem		fúhwe	nifúhwe	kúilifúhwe	icaafúhwe	caafúhwe	tortoise
Variable-stem (restricted)		bemba	nibemba	múilibemba	icaabemba	cáábemba	lake
Subsidiary Class Nouns with Lengthened Prefix							
Rising Stem		baa-kohwé	nibáákohwé	kúilibaakóhwé	icaabáákohwé	cáábáákohwé	monkeys
Falling or High Stem		baa-fúhwe	nibááfúhwe	kúilibaafúhwe	icaabááfúhwe	cáábááfúhwe	tortoises
Variable Stem (restricted)		baa-bemba	nibáábemba	múilibaabemba	icaabáábemba	cáábáábemba	lakes

NOTES TO TABLE 1

This table does not give the patterns for every form of noun; the reader is encouraged to expand the table by her/his own observation. People from different parts of the country may use slightly different patterns, although they will probably use more or less the same number of patterns; there may also be mistakes in the table because of inadequate study.

TABLE 2 - NOMINAL PREFIXES AND DEMONSTRATIVES

Class	Noun prefixes (unstable): full form	short form	(stable): indefinite form	e- form (definite)	tee- form (negative)	Adjectives: -suma (good)	-mbi (other)	Demonstratives: (this nearer)	(that further)	Possessive pre-prefix
1	umu-	mu-	muu-	emu-	teemu-	umu-sumá	'u-mbí	uyú	uyó	uwa-
2	aba-	ba-	baa-	eba-	teeba-	abá-sumá	bá-mbí	abá	abó	abaa-
3	umu-	mu-	muu-	emu-	teemu-	u'u-sumá	'u-mbí	uyú	uyó	uwa-
4	imi-	mi-	mii-	emi-	teemi-	i'i-sumá	'í-mbi	i'í	iyó	iya-
5	i-[1]	i-	lii-	e-	tee-	ili-sumá	li-mbi	ili	ilyó	ilya-
6	ama-	ma-	maa-[2]	ema-	teema-	ay'á-sumá	y'á-mbi	ay'á	ay'ó	ay'aa-
7	ici-	ci-	cii-	eci-	teeci-	ici-sumá	ci-mbi	ici	icó	icaa-
8	ifi-	fi-	fii-	efi-	teefi-	ifí-sumá	fí-mbi	ifi	ifyó	ifya-
9	iN-[3]	N-	niN-	eN-	teeN-	i'i-sumá[5]	'i-mbi	i'í	iyó	iya-
10	iN-[4]	N-	niN-	eN-	teeN-	ishí-suma[5]	shi-mbí	ishi	ishó	ishaa-
11	ulu-	lu-	luu-	elu-	teelu-	ulu-sumá	lu-mbí	ulú	uló	ulwa-
12	aka-	ka-	kaa-	eka-	teeka-	aká-sumá	ká-mbi	aká	akó	akaa-
13	utu-	tu-	tuu-	etu-	teetu-	utu-sumá	tu-mbí	utú	utó	utwa-
14	ubu-	bu-	buu-	ehu-	teehu-	ubii-sumá	bii-mbi	uhú	ubó	ubwa-
15	uku-	ku-	kuu-	eku-	teeku-	ukú-sumá	ka-mbí	ukú	ukó	ukwa-
16						apá-sumá	pá-mbí	apá	apó	apaa-
17						ukú-sumá	ká-mbí	ukú	ukó	ukwa-
18						umú-sumá	mú-mbí	umú	umó	umwa-

NOTES TO TABLE 2
(See number references in the table)

1 Most nouns in class 5 have the prefix *i-*, but words with a stem beginning in a vowel (like *ili-ino,* 'tooth') or in a nasal compound (like *ili-ngala.* 'feather') have the prefix *ili-*. Some speakers also use this prefix for nouns with a one-syllable stem (like *ili-bwe,* 'stone'), but other speake s say *i-bwe*.

2 This form of the prefix may run together with a stem beginning with a vowel, e.g. *meeno* (from *maa-ino*), 'they are teeth'; this form is then the same as the short form, except that the tone-pattern is frequently different.

3 This prefix is spelt with a capital *N* to show that it may take a number of forms such as *in-, im-, iŋ-,* depending on the following sound (see page 5). A few words in class-pair 9/10 can have a plural class 10 prefix *ishaN-,* for instance *i!shamfumu,* 'chiefs' – really the class 10 possessive pre-prefix.

4 See previous note for *N*. Nouns in class-pair 11/10 with a one-syllable stem like *ulu-pwa,* 'family' have a plural class 10 prefix *indu-,* e.g. *indu-pwa* 'families'. This is really the class 10 prefix added to the class 11 prefix instead of directly to the stem.

5 Some speakers, including those in the Kasama district, say *in-suma* in place of *i'i-suma* and *ishi-suma*.

TABLE 3 - PRONOMINAL FORMS

Person or Class	Possessive Pronoun stem	Pronoun forms with *na-*. 'with'	'and'	Verbal pronouns: subject	object	Participle prefix
I	-ándí 1	nandi	nainé, neene	na-/ni-/N- 2	-N- 3	
we	-ésú 1	nensú	naifwé, neefwe	tu-	-tú-	
you (familiar)	-óbé 1	noobé	naiwé	u- 4	-ku-	
you (pl./polite)	-énú 1	neenú	naimwé, neemwe	mu-	-mú-	
1	-ákwé 1	nankwé	naó	a-/á 5	-mu-	ú'u-
2	-ábó 1	naabó	nabó	bá-	-bá-	ába-
3	-áúkó		naó-	'ú-	-'ú-	ú'u-
4	-áíkó		nayó	'í-	-'í-	í'í-
5	-álíkó		nalyó	li-	-lí-	ili-
6	-áy'ákó		nayó	y'á-	-y'á-	áy'a-
7	-ácíkó		nacó	cí-	-cí-	ici-
8	-áfikó		nafyó	fí-	-fí-	ifi-
9	-áíkó		nayó	'í-	-'í-	í'í-
10	-áshíkó		nashó	shí-	-shí-	ishí-
11	-álúkó		naló	lú-	-lú-	úlu-
12	-ákákó		nakó	ká-	-ká-	áka-
13	-átúkó		nat ó	tú-	-tú-	útu-
14	-ábúkó		nabó	bú-	-bú-	úbu-
15	-ákúkó		nakó	kú-	-kú-	úku-
16	-ápákó		napó	pá-	-pá-	ápa-
17	-ákùkó		nakó	kú-	-kú-	úku-
18	-ámúkó		namó	mú-	-mú-	úmu-

52

NOTES TO TABLE 3

1. The tones marked are those used in the short and stable forms; in the full form the last tone is low, e.g. *icítabo cándí* 'my book', *í!cándi* 'mine'.

2. The prefix varies according to what comes after it; if it is followed by a tense sign beginning in *a* it is *na-;* if it is followed by *-ingá-* or the subjunctive negative *-i-*, it is *ni-;* otherwise it is *N-* (that is, any nasal consonant depending on the following sound). Special things happen in tenses with a tense prefix; instead of *naa + N-* we get *niN-*, e.g. *nímfiká* 'I've arrived', and instead of *a + N-* in the hypothetical tenses we have simply *N-*, e.g. *mbá niné* 'if it were me'.

3. *-N-* means any nasal consonant according to the following sound – see the table on page 2. Before an imperative, some speakers say *niN-* instead of *N-*, e.g. *nimpééníkó fwaka*, 'give me some tobacco'.

4. Some speakers say *nuu-* instead of *naa+u-*, e.g. *núúfiká* or *náaúfiká*, 'you have arrived'.

5. The prefix is *a-* if the next two tones are low and then high; otherwise it is *a-*, but in that case the next tone is made high. Examples: *ákafúmáko*, 'he will come from there', *akáfikakó* 'he will arrive there'. The prefix disappears if there is a tense prefix or negative prefix, for instance *nááfiká* 'he has arrived', *talaafika*, 'he has not arrived yet'.

TABLE 4a - SIMPLE AND CONTINUOUS ACTIONS (BOUND)[1]

Distant past *kale* some days ago	Further past *mailo* yesterday	Nearer past *leelo* earlier today	Present *nomba* just now	Immediate future *nomba* shortly	Further future *mailo* tomorrow
Simple actions: affirmative					
-a'- -ILe[2]	-a'- -ILe-[3]	-aci- -a	-a'- -a[4]	-alaa'- -a	-ka- -a
they sewed *báábililé*	*báábilile*	*báácíbíla*	*báábila*	they will sew *báálaábila*	*bákábila*
they washed *báacápilé*	*báácápile*	*báácícápá*	*báácápá*	they will wash *báálaacápá*	*bákacápá*
Simple actions: negative					
ta- -a'- -ILe	ta- -a'- -ILe	ta- -aci- -a		ta- -a'- -e	ta- -aka- -e
they did not sew *tabáábililé*	*tabáábilile*	*tabáácíbila*		they will not sew *tabáábilé*	*tabaakabilé*
they did not wash *tabáacápilé*	*tabáácápile*	*tabáácícápá*		they will not wash *tabaacápé*	*tabaakacápé*
Continuous actions: affirmative					
-alee'- -a	-alee'- -a	-acilaa'- -a	-lee'- -a[5]	-alaa'- -a	-kalaa'- -a
they were sewing *báaléébila*	*bááléébila*	*báácíláábila*	they are sewing *báléébila*	they will be sewing *báálaábila*	*bákalaábila*
they were washing *báaléecápá*	*bááléécápá*	*báácíláacápá*	they are washing *báléecápá*	they will be washing *báálaacápá*	*bákalaacápá*
Continuous actions: negative					
ta- -alee'- -a	ta- -alee'- -a	ta- -acilaa'- -a	ta- -lee'- -a[5]	ta- -alee'- -a	ta- -akalee'- -a
they were not sewing *tabáaléébila*	*tabááléébila*	*tabáácíláábila*	they are not sewing *tabáleebila*	*tabaaléébila*	*tabaakaléébila*
they were not washing *tabáaléecápá*	*tabááléécápá*	*tabáácíláacápá*	they are not washing *tabáleecápá*	they will not be washing *tabaaléecápá*	*tabaakaleecapa*

An apostrophe is used to show tense-signs that do not run together with a following vowel (see page 8).

54

NOTES TO TABLE 4a

1 The corresponding unbound tenses have the feature of diatony, except where a special tense is given in the notes.

2 The corresponding unbound tense is *–ali- -lle* e.g. *báalífikílé* (they arrived long ago), *báalífumíné* (they left long ago)

3 The corresponding unbound tense is *–alii'- -a* e.g. *báálíífiká* (they arrived yesterday), *báálíifúmá* (they left yesterday).

4 The corresponding unbound tense is *–a'- -a* e.g. *bááfiká* (they have just arrived), *bááfuma* (they have just left). This pair of tenses covers both things that are on the point of happening, e.g. *naaísá* (I'm just coming).

5 This tense is also used for acts to take place later in the day, whether simple or continuous.

TABLE 4b
PERFECT AND HABITUAL TENSES

BOUND TENSES		
-ILe	*-a'- -a*	*-a*
bákoséshé umúténgó they have raised the price	*báákuulá ínŋandá* they have built a house	*bálúka ámatanda* they make mats
bákáfishé ámenshí they have heated the water	*báafúlá isémbé* they have forged an axe	*bábúmbá ímitondo* they make pots
UNBOUND TENSES		
naa- -a	*-ali- -a*	*-la- -a*
umúténgó náaúkosá the price is high	*báalíshípá* they are brave	*bálápéépá* they take tobacco
ubwáli náabúkábá the nshima is hot	*báalíkúlá* they are grown up	*bálapépá* they are religious
NEGATIVE TENSES		
ta- -ILe	*ta- -a'- -a*	*ta- -a*
umúténgó taúkóselé the price is not high	*tabááshipá* they are not brave	*tabápeepá* they do not take tobacco
ubwáli tabúkábilé the nshima is not hot	*tabáakúlá* they are not grown up	*tabápépá* they are not religious

The perfect tenses in the first column refer to how things are at the moment; those in the second column refer to how things may be expected to remain. The habitual tenses in the third column refer to things that happen regularly or all the time.

56

www.ingramcontent.com/pod-product-compliance
Lightning Source LLC
Chambersburg PA
CBHW050541270326
41926CB00015B/3334